Woman
of
Options

AN AWAKENING TO THE
POSSIBILITIES OF PURPOSE

MONIQUEA MATTHEWS

Greatness Discovered
PUBLISHING
From pen to published

Greatness Discovered Publishing
P.O. Box 58091
New Orleans, LA 70158
Phone: 504-556-2234
www.greatnessdiscoveredpublishing.com

Text design and Book Cover Design by Charlyn Samson

**All scripture quotations, unless otherwise indicated,
are taken from The Holy Bible.**

ISBN: 978-0-578-30932-3 (paperback)

To my Girls

To my girls with options: Nevaeh and Marley, everything I am and strive to be is because of you two. On days I felt like giving up, you remind me of why I first started. You were here for each and every chapter, you witness my transition and commitment to God. I hope when life tries you, you reflect on this very moment and choose the greatest option you will ever have. Losing your life to find it through Christ just like mommy. I love you.

This book is for the woman who is doing everything but still feels empty. To the woman who is seeking purpose in all that she does. To the woman who has been tied to the wrong man, who helped her to forget who she was. To the woman who knows a 9-5 is not who God has created her to be. I love you; I see you, and know you have OPTIONS.

Contents

Introduction

But when they deliver you up, take no thought how or what ye shall speak: for it shall be given to you in that same hour what ye shall speak. For it is not ye that speak, but the Spirit of your Father which speaketh in you. Matthew 10:19-20 KJV

I chose this scripture because I often struggled with writing this book. That is because at one point I did not believe I could be who God has called me to be. I did not believe because I had a lack of faith in God. I never knew how to totally submit to God because I was used to doing things my way, on my terms.

Now, it is time to share, motivate and inspire as many people as I can. I believe Gods' word is true and I'm trusting Him to fill and empower me to reach you.

I know you have a story too. This is your moment to let it out. If you haven't already, do so now. Don't worry about yesterday. Don't worry about tomorrow. Let's live in today. You are here, right here, in this moment in time, right where you should be. God has already given you all that you need for this moment.

Music has always been a part of my life. When I listen to a favorite song (I have a lot of them), I usually see myself living out my dream life. I am a visual person and I constantly see myself in the best of any song. The vision that God gave to me comes alive when certain songs play, while other songs are confirmation that what I may be feeling is normal and God has a plan bigger than what I can see. I believe I have a gift of taking any song and breaking it down into a life lesson. Gospel music helped me to understand the bible before I understood how to read it. It has always been my calm in the storm, from my father coming home drunk filled with anger, to after his death, and while I'm trying to navigate through life as a new mom. Gospel music was my comfort after I moved into my first apartment outside of Chicago. I remember feeling afraid and alone while my daughter and I ate dinner on the floor because we had no furniture. It was my calm then; it is my calm and therapy now. Gospel music is my ministry, it is my original scripture, Gospel music just makes sense to me.

As you continue to read this book you will see I mention songs in each chapter. That is because most of the songs helped me through many dark nights. I believe in our worship is where chains are being broken and a new layer of us is coming through. I would love for you to listen to each song as they come up in each chapter to get a better feel of the Woman of Options Movement. Also, you will see throughout the book, the Moniquea Musing (M.M). These are my reflections as I journey through this book.

*Tasha Cobbs Leonard sings a song
entitled - Wonderful Grace*

I often cry as the song plays. Yes, I have heard it over a thousand times, but for some reason today I felt the need to share it with you. It does not matter what you have done or how long it has taken you to start what God has called you to do. Maybe you are not sure of what your purpose is and what you are called to do. He still loves you and His grace will always reach you. I believe by the end of this book you will come to terms with who you are and what God has given you.

I pray this message reaches you right where you are and it leaves you feeling awakened, empowered, and motivated.

Chapter One

FATHER WOUND

As I'd began to heal, I could only think
about my father and our relationship.
I had to look back to understand how
I have gotten to this place. M.M.

Little girl with the daddy wound
Do you not know you have the father of all fathers?
Do you not know He is waiting for you?

You must let the pain go and heal.
You must let the pride go and forgive.

It's more to you than what you've been through.
Know that God has a plan for you.

So, what are you going to do?
Hold on to the grudge and live-in regret
or will you forgive and never forget.

Use your experience to bless another.
It's all a part of the test to help heal one another.

Let God use you to plant a seed
but first, you have to dig up your weeds.

There's greatness on the other side, see?
You can get it if you only believe.
You can get it if you're open to receive.
God knows your desires and every need, just ask Him to guide your feet.

The one thing we all have in common is we all have the father of all fathers, and He is known to heal all wounds. M.M.

This chapter almost became a father bashing segment. I almost went in for the kill on my daddy, headfirst. But, once again God stepped right on in and got me straight. He said, "umm, no ma'am, there is more to your father than what you believe." At that moment, He gave me a revelation of my father and how things may have felt on his behalf. See, it is easy to put the blame on someone else for our life and short comings. Granted, this chapter is about my father and our relationship, but I am a grown woman now with kids of my own. I cannot be out here playing the blame game. I have to choose to be who God created me to be and heal so I can make a way for all the women who are coming behind me.

My father was a Vietnam Veteran who did not take any stuff from no one, not even his mother, sad to say. He was a man of few words but when he spoke, you had no choice but to stop and listen. For the most part, he was very humble, hardworking, and minded his business. He and my mother married in the mid 70s and his family gave him a very hard time about that. My mom came from a poor family. She and majority of her siblings were high school dropouts. My mother was dark-skinned, and my dads' side was half white. So, you can only image that there was a lot of colorism in my family. My father received a lot of pull back for marrying my mother. He was asked "How are your kids going to benefit from this?" If the mother was dark, uneducated, and poor then that means her children would be also. There were even comments like, "Matthews' are supposed to be light-skinned, not dark." My dads' side was self-centered and very judgmental. My dad began to resent his family and stayed to himself. Instead of carrying us to victory, he would come home angry and drunk. My father had begun to doubt himself and his kids. He believed he had failed his kids and his kids had failed him. He grew to become insecure about his wife because he was missing the approval of his family. I think, if he had the support of his family, maybe he could have confidently supported us in a loving, supportive way. I also believe deep down he may have believed the negative things not realizing it was hurting and traumatizing to us as children and even into adulthood.

> We are capable of doing whatever we are meant to do, we just needed his support as our father, period. M.M.

I used to be so happy to have my mom and dad in one household, but what good is that if your dad is not emotionally or even sometimes physically there? I grew to love the sound of a lawn mower early in the morning. I am not sure if it is because I am an outside kind of girl or because it was the morning after my dad had been fussing, fighting, and cursing that he would be outside working like a peaceful, hardworking father. It was like the perfect Saturday to wake up to the sound of the lawn mower, the smell of my mom's breakfast cooking, and Saturday morning cartoons. I felt like a normal kid with a normal family. But, as soon as he finished mowing the lawn he would be gone. There were no good mornings, no kiss on the cheek, or any fatherly love. In fact, I've never seen my mom and dad kiss or hug, ever. No one on my dads' side of the family ever showed any affection. It was very difficult and confusing in my home growing up. During the day, it was like a beautiful Spring Easter Sunday. Green grass, bright colorful flowers, and a clear blue sky. My dad would wake up early for work, take me to school, and give me money when I needed it. He was a very good provider. We never went without food or worried about something being turned off. At night, however, it was literally like hell on earth. We would not see him until maybe nine at night, or later and he would be good and drunk by then. There was never a night he did not stay out to drink. He had this certain entrance tone when he came home. It was like a great, big "BOOM!" Then he would start yelling. He would go straight to the point, holding nothing back. I strongly believed he saved everything that was bothering him until he was intoxicated. He would then say what was really on his mind. A lot of times it was very hurtful and very painful. My siblings and I all had our moments where we would cry or argue our need for his approval in our own way. There were plenty of nights where I would wake up to my dad threatening to take my mother's life. In my 5-year-old mind, I thought, "I have to stay up and pray" or "I have to make sure she is safe." It came to the point where I could not go to sleep until I heard my dad snoring. Then I would cry and pray myself to sleep. In fact, going straight to sleep is something that I still struggle with to this day. I often referenced this scripture:

Weeping may endure for a night, but joy comes in the morning" Psalms 30:5b NKJV

This was my everyday life and I learned to adapt very quickly. I remember thinking, "if we could just make it through tonight, everything will be ok in the morning. He would be sober, and the daylight would represent life, a new day." It is still my motto to this very day. The good thing about nights like that was I felt closer to God. Looking back, I always had a friend in Jesus.

I honestly believe if I did not have a certain fear of my dad, I would not have known God like I did. M.M.

My mom taught me how to pray at a very young age. I am not totally sure why she did not teach my other siblings. Maybe because I was curious about God. I had a lot of compassion and believed in always doing what was right. I was always searching for answers of what I could do to make my dad more peaceful. I also think my mom was tired of how things were and had to do something different. She would tell me to pray and rebuke the mean and evil words my dad would say. I have always been different from my siblings. I am the youngest of eight and have always been wise beyond my years. It is something that I still struggle with to this day. Wishing I had someone who I could talk to who really understands me. Someone who can pour into me the same way that I pour into others. A lot of times, I have conversations that compliment my sibling's choice, certain topics of conversation just to talk with them. I am now learning how to walk in who God has created me to be. I have decided not to lower myself just to talk to anyone, just to feel a part of something. It kind of reminds me of Tasha Cobbs Leonard's I Have Decided

I have decided to follow Jesus
'Cause He never ever led me astray

No turning back
The cross before me
The world behind me

This is one of the reasons I have decided to take up Gods' request to write this book. It is almost like a sign or as if I had no other choice. I have no one to talk to, so I have to write it down to get it out, which ultimately led me to healing. Even when I may disobey and decide to talk to someone about something, I often regret the conversation. I would immediately realize God had already given me the answer and that person only made me feel bad and to be bring me back to my God-given answer. As I write this, I also realize that maybe I was addicted to the pain that brings me to the process. I was addicted to feeling hurt in order to make a move towards something that I know I should do. It is like I know they cannot give me the answer, but I must share it with them anyway. Once I am done, I feel horrible and then I go ahead and do what had already been given to me to do. I know I am now jumping ahead of myself, so allow me to give a snippet about how God requested me to write this book and as you continue to read chapter one you will see why I may have been addicted to the pain of conversation.

After many tears and prayers God finally answered me in 2019 of what my purpose was. I was sleeping in my bed, and He woke me and said, "create books and films based on your dreams and experiences." I held that near and dear to my heart and thought about it constantly, but I never considered myself to be a writer. It is now 2021 and I am in the process of completing this book. One of the reasons I think I may have taken as long as I did to write this book is because I felt the things, I believed in did not matter. This goes back to my childhood which is why we are starting with the father wound. We all know fathers are a girls' first love. They are our security, protection, and they are supposed to equip us with the tools needed for the world. I remember telling my dad my dreams and views of the world and he would basically dismiss them. I understand now, after many tears and a revelation from God that he did not believe the cycle could be broken. I was never afraid to ask my dad for anything, unlike my other siblings who would stay out of his way. He would say things like, "you are the only one who needs everything, you are not like the other kids, you are all talk, none of the other kids talk about the things you talk about. They did not ask for the things you are asking for. How are you going to do the things you are talking about? It is not possible, if I or your siblings could not do it, how can you? I cannot support you because I've never seen it be done before." All of those comments were his fears and what he was conditioned to believe. They all came from his family, the time and place in which he was born (1946, Mississippi), and serving in the Vietnam War. Now you may begin to see why I was addicted to the pain of conversation. For years his actions and tolerance towards me, hurt me very deeply but for some reason I always had a sense of hope and desire for something more than what he said I could have. I believe I was challenging him too much and he just wanted things to be as is. He was the type of old school parent that believed these are the cards we were dealt, so leave it alone. Just go to school and come home, no extra curriculum activities. Which is interesting because he always stressed and fussed about, "being somebody", whatever that meant. My dad always stressed how important it was to be successful and go to college, but he was never there to check my homework. As a child, I thought my dad was very smart, but I never heard him read, ever. I do believe he was a smart man, but he never took the time to teach me anything academically. Since my mom was not well educated, homework was not necessarily a must. So, I pretty much was in control of my learning ability. All of this eventually turned into resentment towards him and everyone that was attached to him, including my siblings. I grew the mentality of, "I am going to do things my way and not be like any of you", not even my mom. I thought, "I could do what I wanted to do and just ask God to bless it. I am right for feeling the way I am feeling and none of you will ever understand." All of this is why it was hard for me to submit to God, but we will get to that in another chapter.

Looking back now, I know my dad was struggling, not only financially but spiritually too. I believe he was suffering from a mother wound because he had little patience with her even if he was sober. He would curse her out and never took any of her advice. Family members said my grandmother was mean, however, I never experienced that with her. I find this to be interesting because when I tell people about my father, they would often say, "he was cool to me."

I love my father dearly and I believe if it was not for his tough love and his strength, I would not be the woman I am today. It is not always about us and what someone has done to us. We do not realize as kids that we are watching our parents grow right before our eyes. They are not just raising us; they are growing as well. They are trying to figure things out. It is unfortunate that most of their decisions will affect us in some way. But as women, mothers, and children of God, we have options. We have to decide to let go and let God. My father was a broken man trying to raise kids. No, it is not a good mixture, but this should not be just about how terrible someone's father is, but to acknowledge that there are a lot of broken men out there. They need to know they have options too, but it begins with us as mothers, sisters, and wives to heal first in order to motivate our families.

This thing is bigger than us. M.M.

I can only imagine how hard it may have been for my father. That is why it is so important to have a relationship with God. No matter what others may think, you have to know who you are and who God has created you to be. You cannot take others' opinions and fears and create a life out of it. God created you for His purpose and glory alone. I believe if my dad would have had a better relationship with God, he would have had a better relationship with his wife and kids no matter what his family may have thought. A clear vision of who he was and how to understand his kids.

With this understanding, I thank God that I have a relationship with Him, and I am trying my best to have a great relationship with my kids and teach them the importance of waiting on God. This world is evil and self-righteous, and we all need God, we need our creator to keep us on the right path because it is easy to become bitter and angry. We cannot lose sight of the bigger picture of why we are here.

As we move on to the next chapter, reflect on the father wound poem from the beginning of this chapter. Most of us have a father wound. Some are too ashamed to admit it and others are too caught up in their ways to heal it. Which one are you? Is there something God has called you to do but you do not feel worthy or qualified? Is there someone you need to forgive? Is there any pain that you are holding on to? It is okay to go back to get an understanding of your past so you can heal for the future. Just do not stay there too long. We are waiting for you, we need you.

Chapter Two

WHY DO WE WANT TO BE IN A RELATIONSHIP

Have you ever wanted something so bad that you'll do whatever to get it?
And once you get what you think you wanted,
you realize much later, you always had what you needed?

You realize the one person who will never leave you nor forsake you has always been there waiting for you to invite Him to do life with you

If this is you, don't worry
I've made this mistake too
The good news is God forgave us before we made any mistakes

He's now waiting for us to invite Him in. M.M.

Remember in the first chapter I talked about how I started to resent my father and decided I was not going to be like him, or anyone attached to him? Well, that is exactly what I tried to do.

My mother had been battling cancer since I was in the 7th grade. She was my best friend. I could tell her anything and she always gave the best Godly advice. She passed away when I was in the 11th grade. I took it very hard. The one person who understood me and allowed me, to be my goofy self is now gone. I often told myself, "I cannot talk to my father because he doesn't understand, plus he is always gone every weekend with his girlfriend." So, I quickly surrounded myself with people who helped me to forget the pain. Let me take a moment to be honest, I always wanted to be in an exclusive relationship. That was the ultimate goal for me. I believed that was the answer to all my problems; find a man who will love me, go to work and we go to church every Sunday. Oh, yea, he wouldn't drink either.

In 2020, I ended an 11year relationship with my kid's father. As I was beginning to heal, I often thought about what my future husband would be like? I could not help but wonder when would I meet him? One night I was laying in my bed around 2am and these words came to me:

> So, you want to be in a relationship? First off, why do you want to be in a relationship? What's your why? Ok, don't tell me yet. After you get your answer, understand you were created on purpose with a purpose in the mind of God - It was not an accident. You are breathing so that means He is requiring something of you. Someone needs you and I do not mean a relationship. Someone needs you to start that business, blog, or class.

> Sometimes we get into the wrong relationship and as women, we have big hopes that it will work out how we planned it in our heads. And when things begin to fall apart, we then lose focus of who we are and what really matters. God will always give you what you need. That means your husband will find you at the right place and at the right time. You cannot expect to find your husband while having the same mindset you have now. You must know who you are in order to know who is meant to be in your life. We must make sure what we currently want is aligned with our destiny. Sometimes what we want is only temporary and is not what we will want 5 years from now or it is not what God designed for us to have.

> For an example, what if now you have a thing for bad boys and your man sells drugs (do people still sell drugs?) And

your hopes are, he will soon stop and begin to go to church and marry you. Now all those things are very possible right, but what if that is not what he wants and all of what you think he could be? So, God has called you to open an all-girls school, charity, foundation for abused girls and some of those girls' moms, dads, are abusers or were drug addicts. You begin to grow in wisdom and empathy for these girls, but your small-minded man thinks this is all he knows or worst, he stalls you from following your dream to begin with? He fails to understand your dreams and thinks it is not possible to have what you desire. Now you have to break this soul tie and do this process all over again to find God where you left Him, find peace, dream again, and live out that dream. All of that can take time. Trust me, I know.

One thing I have realized is you have to be intentional. Intentional with your life, your relationships/ friendships, and even job opportunities. You cannot be out here dating and befriending just anybody. You have to think, "what I'm doing, is it aligned with what God has for me?" "Are the people around me helping me or hindering me?" You cannot allow any and every one into your life and then think you will flourish or think you will get married.

So, to answer the question of why you want to be in a committed relationship, first you must know yourself and what God created you to do. Your soulmate will fall into your purpose naturally, how God intended. But you cannot get any 'ole man when you do not know yourself and try to mold him to fit. You must spend time alone and learn to love yourself.

So, this is what I would like you to do:

Seek God
Get to know yourself
Make peace with your past
Live and grow in your purpose
Become what you want to attract
Be intentional with your relationships
Finally, your soulmate will find you after you find yourself
and you are living in your purpose through God.

You are worth more than just being a girlfriend, friend with benefits, or wife, ok! There is more to you than cooking, washing clothes, or cleaning up. God is powerful and He created us to do great things so we have to tap into that and begin the process before we can think about attaching ourselves to someone else. M.M.

When God gave me those words and understanding, I immediately changed my ideas about relationships and began to work on healing and my purpose.

Imagine attending an event or business party and you are flourishing in conversation with someone whom you have never met before. You look over to your friends or partner and they are looking at you like, "wow, she's talking about things that she doesn't discuss with me." You then say to the person, "I'm sorry, excuse me for a moment." and go back over to your friends or partner to try to make them feel comfortable. You attempt to meet them at their level. They will say, "I see you over there talking, why don't you talk like that with me?"

This is an example of what I often dealt with in my past relationships. What comes to your mind when you think of this example?

I think either my friend or partner should get into the conversation. If they are unable to, we should try to analyze why not. I do not believe your partner or friends should make you feel bad because you are growing and changing for the better. To me that is a good sign that you are not on their level. Maybe you have outgrown them or maybe you were never on their level.

I understand that the following experiences I am about to share with you is not entirely my fault because he chose to do the things with me, however I must share it with you for healing and accountability purposes.

Soul-ties are real. Despite how you may view it, it is indeed real. I met my kids' father a week after I buried my mother through mutual friends. Instead of me being intentional with my life, I was seeking validation from guys. I initiated everything from the very beginning even to my first pregnancy. I wanted to give love the way my mother gave love to me. Also, because I was not receiving the love, I thought I needed from my father. I should have used that time to focus on God.

In order for us to heal and grow we have to acknowledge our part in all situations. M.M.

I remember breaking up with him many times before because I knew deep down, he was not the one, but I was attached on so many levels. If I had put all my focus on God when my mom died, I would have known that he was not the one from the very beginning. He did not have a vision and even though I tried, I could not mold him to be the man I needed. Honestly, neither one of us knew what we needed at that time. So, I have taken ownership and asked God for forgiveness. I have even asked him for forgiveness.

If I would have at least taken time to get to know him, I'm sure we would have ended way before it started. M.M

The good news is God gave us the spirit of power and a sound mind. So, we can be freed from bondage. To break a soul-tie, it will require a move of God, but we will be able to live out our purpose in the end. God forgave us, now we have to do the soul work and forgive ourselves.

When you have a relationship ordained by God you will still live out your purpose, not get stuck or become co-dependent. M.M.

One thing I realized while being in that relationship is kids should not need relationship counseling. Yes, I do believe we all need mentors and therapy, but not relationship counseling for boyfriend and girlfriend relationships. I just do not believe kids should tie themselves so early in life. I believe when a person shows you who they are, you have to believe it. We have our whole lives to live, why do we feel it is more valuable when we are attached to someone?

My first mistake was when he and I broke up in 2012. He was trying to get me back, so I said let's talk to someone. Well, that someone happened to be the man who was raising him. He knew his financial situation. He knew how important it was to step up when you have a kid. Simply put, he knew my ex. I understand now if he couldn't mold him or train him, what makes me think I can? What makes me think he will change? I almost feel like he was using me. It was like he saw something in me he wanted and just wanted to be a part of my life in some way. And being that I was never intentional before and hated being alone, I could not get rid of him completely. We both shared the same kind of pain, and we were attracted to each other but honestly, we didn't match and there was no vision. And the fact that we shared the same pain is a red flag within itself. As we've gotten older, he always felt that I was changing him. That's because he was not supposed to fit into my world, so the adjustment was hard for him. See, a man will take all the things you desire and the things you tell him and try to become that, until he gets to the point where he is tired of pretending.

In a healthy God ordained relationship you will change as you grow in your purpose, together. M.M.

In 2014, two years after my father had passed away, my oldest daughter and I moved to Chicago. I got an apartment and spent most of the days at my sisters' apartment because I couldn't stand to be alone. I often called my kids father to talk about him moving in with me. I did pray and played a lot of gospel music, but I never once attempted to seek God's face. I never once asked what He required of me during that tough season. I hated Chicago so much and constantly complained instead of making things better through Christ. Remember, I never fully healed from my parents' death.

I was always a loner and felt misunderstood. I would always wonder "why am I alone" instead of seeking God and who He had created me to be. My kids father made it easy to be with him because I was trying so hard not to be like my family. I was trying to create my own life. He didn't know what he wanted, he didn't have a vision and didn't have any serious relationships before me. All of this made it easy to set the tone of our relationship.

I remember when I used to be proud to tell people he and I had relations within a week of us dating, like that is something to brag about. It was my way of saying "if y'all are meant to be, it'll be, we had relations the first week we have gotten together and we been together 10 years." That was one of the craziest things I have ever said. I regret all those times I have ever said that. I realize now, my words have power. I realize now that people value my opinion more than I may have noticed before. People do not always take the full advice. They tend to take bits and pieces or the part that kind of gives them the okay to do what they want to do anyway. I realize now I have to use my words to lift women up. I have to say what I mean and mean well. I must use my words to make sense of what God has created us to do. Not use it for foolishness. Just because you have been with someone for a while does not make them God sent. Especially, if you have relations before marriage. On top of that, we have to qualify these men and put God first from the very beginning.

As I stated before, when we met, I was 17 years old after the loss of my mom. I shouldn't have been having relations with anyone.

You give the wrong man sex before
marriage and you'll be stuck with him
forever, it's called soul-ties. M.M.

Then one day you will wonder "how did I get here?" "Why are things not working for me.?" We try so hard not to be like our parents or other family members that we begin to live the cycles we have been trying to avoid.

Also, we should not want to get married for the sake of getting married. God created us with purpose and a vision in mind. And anything that does not align with that we should let go. For years I've tried to make our relationship work and failed to realize the natural state of the relationship did not align with God's vision. I also realized I was becoming that person I've been avoiding or praying not to become.

We must constantly seek God and live
in our purpose, on purpose. M.M.

If we are not careful the enemy will use our weakness against us. We must acknowledge God at all times. When we seek Him, He will make us stronger in our identity. Once He does, we must remain intentional to protect our (His) vision of us, work hard no matter where we are, help others, and remain productive.

I remember growing up, I believed looking in the mirror, was me looking at God. I realize now, it is.

Here is an affirmation I want you to repeat:

> *He lives in me.*
> *I am made in His image.*
> *I try and want to be a reflection of Him every day.*
> *When people see me I want them to see less of me and more of Him.*
> *Today I see there's a change in my reflection.*
> *I believe, I'm glowing.*
> *I believe, I'm changing.*
> *I'm stronger, wiser.*

I don't know about you, but after 11 years, I don't want the wrong soul attached to mine. I don't want my identity hidden again. I know it may sound like witchcraft, but soul-ties are a serious thing. It's meant to keep you from what God created you to do. It's meant to blind you and lie to you.

At the end of 2018, we moved to New Orleans, and we had just had our second daughter. I had this weird feeling in my spirit, it was like I had been sleeping with the enemy. I began to realize I was turning 30 in a few years and have not done anything life changing or purpose driven. I did not like the fact that I was unmarried and doing all the things I was taught not to do, like shack up and have kids out of wedlock. I needed to know if we were meant to be and if I should stay. In 2019 my sister told me to pray and asked God to reveal his truth. A few weeks later, I found out he made a baby on me when I was pregnant the year before. Now, when I prayed to God about revealing his truth, I ask Him to give me the peace, strength, and courage I needed to keep moving forward to what He had for me, no matter what He reveals. God did just that. I mean when I found out, I was so calm, I confused myself. I didn't move as quickly as I should have, so the confusion sat in. We all know nothing about God is confusing. It was so bad that I was in communication with the woman and calling myself a stepmom. It took me almost a year to leave and stay gone. I remember it like it was yesterday, I was scared. I was worried he would hurt me for some reason. He was never abusive before, the enemy wanted me to stay. But I knew I had to leave and fully depend on God.

See there goes that word fear again. When the enemy know there's a calling on your life and he sees you are trying to make proper changes, he will then use things like fear, doubt, and soul-ties to keep you stuck. Therefore, we should pray intentional prayers, remember our prayer, and consider it all- take into consideration everything that will take place at the very moment you pray and decide to follow Christ.

We must be ready when we pray. M.M.

Now we are in 2021. I have been single for almost a year now. I realize and understand I needed to spend time alone with God. It had to be just me and Him. I am learning to love being intentionally alone again and thankful He gave me a second chance.

Someone may say,
I am trying to find my balance
I can't be too closed off, I should be open to date

*I can't be to open to date, I must be submitted, focused on
God*
I can't be too closed off and I can't be too available either M.M.

I get it, it's like how do you know if you're doing the right thing? How will you know if God is getting ready to send your soulmate and you are closed off to everyone? I understand, it's hard but that is why we should be focused on God. I believe at the end of the day after much confusion and stress, that God is not. He will give us exactly what we need when we need it. I think the main thing is we should be open to God and open to receive from Him. He will send everything and everyone we need.

Once we understand we have been attached to the wrong men and there is something greater, beyond, and bigger than us, things will make more sense. We couldn't see it before because we have been blinded by our relationships. We pick the first man that we see because we "have a type" and we create our lives in them when we should create our lives in God, the Creator. God made us for a bigger purpose and we're limiting ourselves with these men that are so called our "type".

We have yet to become who we are. M.M.

Chapter Three

THE JOURNEY

Now that we have acknowledged our childhood wounds and past relationships, we must now take up our cross and walk with Christ. We now understand that He has a plan for us. We are now on the journey towards healing and living out our purpose. God will begin to reveal things to us, and we must be intentional, and it will not be easy. God will show us who we are and what negative things we thought were ok. We have to be ready before He can bless us with His promises, or else we will abuse it and others. Please receive it and learn from it. You will need it; you will need all the lessons you have learned to bless someone else.

For God has not given us a spirit of fear, but of power and of love and of a sound mind. II Timothy 1:7 NKJV

Fear is one of the main reasons we have settled and become stagnate. It was the fear of being alone, that is why we stayed in the relationship so long. It was the fear of change or rejection, that is why we haven't started that business yet. It was all fear and it robbed us of our dreams. The good news is God did not create us in fear. He created us to have power and a sound mind. There is nothing confusing or too hard for our God, so let's trust Him just a little bit more, let's go a little deeper in Him. As you begin to grow in new areas, you will be glad you did. So today, lets decide to let go of fear, breakup with doubt and insecurity so we can heal, grow, and glow into our purpose.

This reminds me of Kirk Franklin's Hello Fear.

Hello Fear,
Before you sit down there's something I need to explain

When I first decided to leave my kids father, I had a dream he bought me to a store (Wal-Mart) for my birthday to ask me to be his wife. He had this big plastic ring holder with a necklace, and he could not seem to open it. He was struggling as I was in front of him waiting to put the ring on. I begin to feel ashamed and afraid that there were too many lights to show how cheap or fake the ring was. He needed scissors to cut the tape and twist tie off. At first people were in awe until it took him so long to open it. I begin to think, "why didn't he have this ready before he began to propose or why didn't he get a better ring with a ring box?" So, I said aloud to the people, "thanks for coming, bye!" We then went to the car and the setting changed to my old church parking lot in Mississippi, and he put the ugliest ring on my finger, it was fake and almost looked rotten. I was not pleased and kind of felt sick to my stomach. I could only think of the women who, at the least had sterling silver rings. He then promised he would get a better one soon. It was not a good feeling at all. I woke up and prayed about it. I can only feel that God was telling me, don't be so caught up in getting married that I would settle for anyone, possibly the wrong one. Or maybe he will try to propose to me just so no one will have me, or that he wants me so bad he will make any promises he knows he will not keep. Maybe it was all of the above. One thing I do know is I am thankful I had that dream because there were a lot of times, I attempted to follow God but later returned back to old habits because it was easier. I had what my pastor would call a "trauma bond".

What God has for you, is for you and no one will get in the way of it but YOU. M.M.

God was warning and revealing to me the things I would give in to in the past. I had to receive it, learn from it and move on. It is not easy to leave a relationship that is based on fears and pain because you become addicted, attached, and dependent.

After our breakup, God delivered me from premarital sex and soul-ties. However, we still lived together for a month or so. There were days he would be nice and there would be days it would be very tense. On the days he was nice, I quickly realized I had to be careful because I have seen how I could mistake his amorous behavior for him loving me and wanting to make it work. This was because of our previous "bond". When in reality, he only wanted to please his pride. I understood that just because God delivered me does not mean I shouldn't be intentional on constantly healing and setting new boundaries. I had to learn that I cannot be my naturally nice self any longer because he thought I would give in and take him back. Plus, he knew my triggers, so I had to guard my heart. The old me would have given in when he would become tensed and ask him what was wrong, which would then lead to me opening my heart and wound. In reality, I hadn't done anything wrong, he just didn't respect my decision and wanted to have things his way. That is why it is important to heal and understand why we allowed certain things in the past.

You can't have any seep holes,
let God fill you. M.M.

Growing up I remember seeing certain types of women that I inspired to be. The type of woman who was God-fearing, had a handsome husband, nice cars, great with money, and knew how to raise their daughters, much like the modern-day Proverbs 31 woman. Somewhere along the way, I lost that vision. I am not sure if I stopped seeing those women or if it was because I was so consumed with what was around me. Maybe I became more insecure, maybe it was both. I began to attach myself with women I was not comfortable with becoming and who would not hold me accountable. I also didn't know how to take proper instructions. I thought I knew everything, and I would get embarrassed and be easily offended. As time went on, I begin to ask God, where are my people? Where are the people you have created for me? He revealed to me that I couldn't be insecure. He said, "When you see the women you wouldn't mind becoming, don't be ashamed. Those are the people you should be around, the ones who will interrupt your habits to unlock your best feature." See, it's the same thing with relationships. You shouldn't nurture the relationship with a person you wouldn't want to become. We also shouldn't spend our time with people who we think we are better than, because we are comfortable there, hiding behind their flaws and internalizing ours. I didn't want to become my ex or the company I was keeping, but I was comfortable because I was embarrassed and insecure of others, the people I should have been around. I started to believe those women were not sincere. I started to believe they were stuck up, but none of that was true. We should choose our mentor and friends based on our vision and what we want to become in the next 5 years. Then, we should listen and take their advice. We have to believe we deserve to be in the room as well, not to step on anyone toes or use their flaws to shine light onto ourselves.

You cannot give everyone your light, not everyone is worthy of what God gave to you. M.M.

The more you try to elevate and live in your purpose, you will see who really has your back and understands you. There were plenty of times when I would wake up feeling bright as the sun. I would feel peace and joy with all the happiness. I would begin to text my siblings but something in me would say, "Girl, keep your joy. As soon as you get a little something, you want to give it right back. Keep your peace and joy cause as soon as I hang up, I would say "why did I call them?" When I would wake up like that, I want to call someone and spread my love and happiness but when I do, they never feel the same and when I hang up, I feel empty. I had to learn to be happy alone and keep my joy. Now don't get me wrong, it is a great thing to spread love, but when you have never been intentionally alone, with God, you tend to pick and choose the wrong group of people in order to feel the love God is waiting to give you Himself. It is something in us that makes us need to be around someone, even if they are not good for us. We have to spend time alone with God to heal so He can make us new and whole.

God will reveal who your real friends are and what kind of friend you are. M.M.

During my time alone with God, I realized that I am not for everyone. I didn't understand this before. However, I did notice it was hard for me to be myself and talk with certain people, including past friends. I was never showing up as my real self. Part of that was because of fear and rejection. I have family members who don't understand me, so what would make my "friends" any different. I felt as though I was being fake with a fake smile. The other part was the fear of offending others because of my walk with Christ. Majority were flat out insecure. I did not always show up for others and was very selfish at times. I now know that for me to have friends, I must first show myself as friendly. I must also vet people and be open to receive good people. After I came to terms with that, I apologized for my inconsistent and selfish ways because it is now time to keep moving forward.

Looking back, I understand I must be consistent and true to who God created me to be. I cannot be afraid to share the Goodness of Jesus in order to make others feel comfortable. Don't let the enemy trick you into believing you cannot move on after you have done wrong.

Now is the time to be intentionally alone to become a better you and fix what you have been conditioned to. M.M.

What do I have to lose? That was the question I had to ask myself. When I decided to follow Christ, abstain from premarital sex, end an 11-year relationship, and stop drinking, people close to me looked at me as though I may have been tripping or confused. They would ask, "are you sure? He's a good father and wants to be there, no one is celibate these days." When you realize the bad out weight the good and that God has all you need, the question becomes "What do I have to lose?" God saved me from myself. I always tried to come up with new ideas and adventures, but He showed me nothing has changed, there was no vision, provision, no savings, investments, nothing. We were basically in the same boat we were in since 2016. What do I have to lose? I have already lost everything. There were times I put him before God, money, my parents, cars, and friends. What else do I have to lose? Yes, he is a good father but that should not change because we are over. I knew in that moment that I had nothing to lose but all to gain. It was time to pick up where I left God and gain everything that was ordained for me. God is all we need, and He will supply all of our needs.

You have nothing to lose, but ALL to gain. M.M.

As we end this chapter, I pray you have all the strength and courage you need to follow God and get the lessons you need because we need you. We are doing this together; it is not a coincidence. Also, this is the only chapter I will be leaving my reflections of what we just covered: Number one, let go of fear. Number 2, we cannot get caught up in wanting to get married because we may choose wrong. Number 3, stay the course, don't return to habits because it is easier. Number 4, let go of shame and the spirit of offence. Number 5, spend time with God to know who is meant for you. Number 6, don't be ashamed to be who God called you to be, it's almost blasphemy. Number 7, and finally, what do you have to lose?

I would like to leave you with another great song, Amen by Anthony Brown because this is my prayer for you.

Chapter Four

AWAKEN

It is Sunday morning, and I am almost finished preparing breakfast for my girls when one of my favorite songs come on, Miracle Worker by Anthony Brown. Little did I know, the song was preparing me for a great word from my Pastor who was preparing me for a great word for you.

Both the song and my Pastors' message reminded me of where I started when I was awakened. It also was a reminder that we should wait on the Lord because nothing is too hard for Him. As we wait, we should not revert back to our old ways. We should be steadfast and claim our territory. Sometimes when a person is awakened, they immediately think everything will automatically start working for them. This is not necessarily true. When I was awakened, the feeling was as if I had reached an epiphany. I began to realize I was doing everything all wrong, and that's ok. When God began to show me a vision of my future, I then decided to follow Him because I knew based on my past choices, I couldn't manifest the vision He gave to me without following Him. With following Him, although God is a miracle worker, things will not happen overnight. With following Him, comes the testing of your faith because He must be sure your heart is right and you will be able to handle the blessings of God, repentance is important because we have made so many mistakes. We should acknowledge them and decide to make a complete change in a new direction, and lastly, time for healing. We must allow God to change our minds, hearts and restore us. All of those are beautiful things and are a part of your journey of being awakened. When or if you have already reached this point, please do not get weary or discouraged, this is why you should remain steadfast because it is a process and you could be closer than you think, hold tight.

I find it very interesting that the devil knows our desires just as well as God does. If we are not careful, he will take something we want, wrap it up, and present it to us. If you haven't been awakened by God, you would not realize that this thing is raggedy and not wrapped properly. If you were like me, at some point you'd take it, love it, and try to make sense of it like it was heaven sent. Oh, but God did not give up on me and He will not give up on you. When He wakes us up, we then realize the enemy took a small portion of what we wanted and wrapped it up to where we could not see clearly. We have to be careful of what we pray for because a lot of times we are picking and choosing the generic brand, the great value version of what God really has for us and we're so anxious that we are selling ourselves short. The great news is, there's no such thing as too late. When God awakens us, we have to take ownership of our part in the situation and move forward with Him.

Recently, I was riding in my car after work. I had so many emotions coming over me and I began to say, "moments like this I wish I had someone to call on who had been there and done that. Someone who is on a higher level than I am and who knows God." Then these words came to me, "Yes, that would be nice to have those kinds of people to call on but if you call on them, you will never call Him" I felt that very deeply in my spirit because I know I will call on them in a heartbeat and then forget who's really the source.

Why would you want the resource when you can have the source? M.M.

I used to get upset that no one was able to give me the advice I believed I deserved. And once I accepted that there was no one who could give me proper advice, I began to praise myself. That was before I was awakened. Now I know no one was able to give me the advice I needed because God was the only one who could deliver me.

God is my therapist. M.M.

I now understand that a lot of my pain and hurt came from self-inflicted wounds. All I had to do was stop and acknowledge God. I was making my life harder than it had to be.

Wake up... Hey, Are you up? Now that He has your attention, don't stay in this bed of defeat for long. If we are not careful, we can damage ourselves, or worse place the opportunity for damage into someone else's hands. M.M.

Damage by H.E.R is one of my favorite songs. If you haven't noticed by now, I have a lot of favorites. What I take from this song is, we are the only one who is in control, besides God. We get to decide who we will let into our lives and to what extent.

I am now awakened, and I will not put my kids through this again. M.M.

When my ex and I called it quits, it seemed as though he was doing everything, he said he would do for his music. He released a mixtape a week after the breakup and was doing interviews. I was not jealous; it was just very difficult. While I was wondering what my kids and I would eat or how I would pay the bills, he is living his life. I felt like he was using me. He was using that time to pay for stuff since he was not paying for many things here. I know I should have been better with my money and not depend on any man and I was working and praying daily to become better. I just hate that he was still there.

During that time, I learned that I have to protect my energy. It makes sense to me now why I always had anxiety. He had this dark strange energy about him that made me feel uncomfortable. I remember times when I would start to feel anxious, I'd go for a ride and immediately start to feel good, and he would call me to see if I was alright because I would be taking my time and enjoying my peace. I also realized I was forced to become a minimalist. I always stated I wanted to be a minimalist, but I never paid attention to the fact that I was low key living like one. I was working with bare minimums and Jesus. Yes, it did hurt, and I cried a lot. I understand now it was molding and teaching me. I will never put me or my kids in the situation again. I had nothing but daycare money in my account with noodles in the cabinet. I began to understand that as women we have to qualify our relationships and live on an intentional budget.

Sometime after that I was able to see my cousins for the first time in a while. It was my first time being sober as an adult. I was able to see how they behaved under the influence. I was always drinking with them and was unintentional with the way I was living when I was in their presence, so I never saw the cycles clearly. Once I was able to observe their behaviors, it quickly helped me to realize I did not want to live a life without God ever again. I don't want to live in my flesh while God rides the back seat as if I was in control. I want God all around me and my kids. I feel free and alive with Him. I'm at peace and have joy. I don't want it any other way. I need Him to fill me and use me. I want people to understand they don't have to stay like this. God has something better for all of us.

Remember who you are, you don't have to prove anything to anybody. M.M.

In case you haven't noticed, I am an introvert. Yes, it took me by surprise too. I love to talk but only to my closest family and friends. Yes, I am loud but again, only with my closest family and friends. I prefer not to meet new people because I rush in my head for the moment when we finally know each other and past the beginning stages. I love my time to think, cry and talk to God. I like to think about my future and my dreams. I don't like big crowds; I hate meetings at work and don't have to be on social media. After people leave my house, I need a whole day at home alone, to regroup. After a big gathering, I'm so hard on myself about what I could have done better or if I opened up too much.

One night my kids' father and I talked more than ever since the breakup. I was not sure if he was thinking I would give in to him or what? But I didn't see anything wrong with being cordial because the tension would be so deep at times. When we were together, we always had moments where we would play old songs that we once loved, it was usually after a big argument to lighten the mood instead of talking about the issue at hand. I understood what he was doing but I also knew I had been rescued by God from the relationship, so I asked him to play Tori Kelly's Dear No One. I then expressed to him how I recently discovered I was an introvert, and his response was, "I needed to find myself. You just weren't acting like one", he continued. I thought, well of course not, we've been together for 11 years and have kids! My reason for sharing this is because I believe God was showing me that he does not know me and didn't care to, especially the new me. See, in the past, when he tried something, like playing old music, that would get a certain reaction from me. It would open me up to the old "good memories" and make me question all the decisions I'd just made. I understand that he could not figure out what I wanted in that moment, so he thought I didn't know myself. He was so caught up in himself to where he thinks we're one in the same.

Years before I wasn't intentional with my relationships and lifestyle, but now I am. I know myself and understand he doesn't fit in the equation; therefore, he thinks I am confused or wanted to make me believe that I'm confused. And that I'm private and only want to share certain things. Little did he understand, I was constantly praying, writing, thinking, planning, and reading. I was doing more during that time than I had done in the past 11 years. I did not have to share it with him because he was no longer in my circle.

Sometime after, I expressed to him that it is not healthy for us to continue to live like we were. He was constantly in and out and it was not good for our girls. I needed to completely heal and grow. I could not do that if he was still living with me and staying out all night. Being human my mind would think of him because he was there. I told him it was best for him to leave. The next day, he woke up and said he was going to look at some places to live. Immediately, the enemy had me feeling scared, afraid of living alone after all these years. But I had to quickly give that to God because I knew He was all I needed, and I knew deep down we were not meant to be together. I had to acknowledge those feelings, emotions, and understand I had been with him since I lost my mom at the age of 17. I became codependent on him. I expressed things to him that no one else knew. I tried to make him the man I thought I needed and now I'm 28 and about to start over with two kids. I did not have a car and I was just starting to grow my savings. I know all of that was working for my good and that was only the beginning of me getting stronger. I just needed God to fill me, continue to help me to grow, and to learn from that situation.

God, I don't ever want to go through this again. Help me. M.M.

Even though I've always known I was different, that alone was not enough. I understand now I have to work a little harder and differently than before, especially if no one around is leading by example or believes in me. I understand now I have to search God for my purpose and being different doesn't mean things will just happen. We should seek God and ask Him to lead us to our purpose and obey what He requires of us in that time. It's not like I was born the best writer, or most confident one in my family. I had to work and heal to become those things, or I would've just been a product of what I see. It's not magic, you have to work for it. The thing that made me different is the idea from God. The thought of being different, the thought of making a change. The vision God gave to me and wanting more than what I see and having faith in

God to make it possible. What makes me different is deciding to do things differently for a different outcome. What makes me different is doing something with that information and more. What makes me different is being the change I want to see.

> We have to work, continue growing, and
> be willing to learn in order to match
> up with what we believe. M.M.

A month later, it was my baby girl's birthday and her aunt reminded me of who I could be as I continued this journey to find myself again. I had shown her and my cousin how the baby took the kitchen cabinet off the hinges and her aunt put it back together with no problem. She then mentioned a Fantasia song, Even Angels. In the song she talks about starting over. Seeing her screw, the cabinet back together reminded me of the girl I used to be and who I could be now. I was the one to try to figure things out, I did not take no for an answer, and would try to fix things. She reminded me that's it's okay and you got this. It's funny because I used to listen to this song and didn't fully understand the purpose of it. I was with my kids' father when this song came out and listening to it makes me feel that I've let a lot of things go. I miss the simple innocent feelings I used to have. It feels good coming back to this song. I know I can't get those years back, but it feels good to start over, like Fantasia said, "I forgot I could live like this." I can take my time; I can do what I want and be free to figure it out. That's a beautiful thing to me. This song speaks to me and my individuality. It makes me feel like I can fly. Like the sky is the limit. I'm free. Life is beautiful and so am I.

There were times I was feeling lonely and wanted to talk to someone. So, if my ex called, I would answer and talk to him. I'd even began calling him more. But after listening to this song, I realized that was defeating the purpose.

Sometimes, it's necessary to not answer the phone unless it's for the girls. I have to be intentional and break these cycles. I have to make a choice and an effort. I broke up with him for a reason and I have to stand behind that. Thank you, Jesus!

Fly ...

Now, it's time I start dressing like the queen I am. I have to own the room until I get in the room I deserve. M.M.

It was time to acknowledge and believe in the ideas God had given me. I have to speak the language and know, where I am now is only temporary. The thoughts, ideas and dreams I have inside is my destiny, it's eternal. I have to understand the job I have right now is only a seed. It's only a seed to sow into my future, get new ideas and set goals. I can't continue to live paycheck to paycheck and expect to get more. I have to pay my tithes, pay my bills, get things I need and live below my means. God did not create me to suffer. I have everything I need on the inside of me. God did not create me to fail and I if make a mistake, it is a lesson. If people don't believe or support you, that just means they don't have a ticket to your future. It's okay, don't lose focus and don't force them to understand. God will send people who are supposed to be with you, and they will get it and help you. What you are imagining is already done, you just have to believe and become aligned with God's vision.

I'm so glad for all of the things I've been through. I wouldn't be who I am today if it wasn't for the things I experienced. By Christ, my eyes are now open and I'm thankful. I am a living testimony, I'm the girl that has been there and done it. I am what I've always searched for or wanted in someone else. God is doing it through me. There is nothing better, as long as I keep my mind on Him, I can do anything.

If ye have faith as a grain of mustard seed, ye shall say unto this mountain, remove hence to yonder place; and it shall remove; and nothing shall be impossible unto you. Matthew 17:20c KJV

There is something about J.J. Hairstons' song, You Deserve It, that makes me feel so good. It helps me to see me in my future as God intended, how God created me to live. I believe it's an image from God. I'm on stage speaking to women like you and me. We're laughing and I'm being myself with God in me. I see a church, a nice car, nice clean white house, and sunny days. It feels SO awesome. Me, our kids, and my husband are so happy to serve God.

As I listen to my Pastor more and more, I realize my dad was saying the same things. The difference is my Pastor doesn't curse and isn't drunk and that's OK. I think that's why it is so important to honor thy mother and father no matter what. Even though my dad had his own struggles, he still wanted the best for his kids. It was hard for me to find the love in the things he was saying, but I understand now or I'm at least trying to.

―――――――――――――――――――

I am now Awakened. M.M.

―――――――――――――――――――

As you already know, I always loved sunny days. A new day filled with joy, hope and breakfast being prepared. Now that I am a mother, every morning I have to open my blinds in hopes of a sunny day. A day where everything makes sense. I'm not living in sin; I'm living in my purpose and serving God. Nothing can get in my way. Remember when it may seem to others that we are not doing our best, God still loves us. Keep going, keep pushing. You don't have to be perfect, just show up for yourself and Him.

Chapter Five

THE POSSIBILITIES
OF PURPOSE

I always thought I could drink, curse, have sex out of wedlock and be labeled a boss. I thought that if I didn't drink or have sex before church that God will not punish me, and I would not be distracted from getting the word for the week. I always thought being successful was having a lot of money, a luxury apartment I can't afford, and an awesome office job. So that's what I began to strive for. I believe that I could be or do whatever I wanted and just pray that God would cover me, and I'll somehow attain this certain level of success. I loved the fact that I can get up at 7am (because I hate waking up early) drink coffee in my cubicle, and go home to do what I wanted - drink, have a kickback or smoke a little and not worry about a drug test since I was hired in. I would go to church on Sunday, I was adamant about that, but I always thought it was hard or uncommon for a girl my age to be into church, never drink and be celibate. God began to show me how other people were living. People who didn't drink and who were awesome, dope people. Men and women who were celibate and waiting for marriage and they were happy and not stressed. I'd never seen any of this before. He showed me people who understood that if they seek God and their purpose, they will have everything they need. This was the old me and now I thank God, I've had the chance to wake up, very similar to the song by Lacrae – Sunday Morning.

People always say, "I will be true to who I am", but do you know who you are? Do you really know why you were created? There's more to your life than what you're seeing right now. It's bigger than you, it's bigger than us. We were created on purpose with a purpose in mind. Honestly, it's not about you or me. You may have kids like me who are watching you. We can't continue to do the things we did before, say the things we may have said before because our words and thoughts have power- that's who we really are. Our old or normal way of thinking has to cease in order to do something we have never done before. We have to die in order to live. What does that mean? Let go of hurt, pain, baggage, negative words, and thoughts and let God use us. That will require less of you and more of Him. So, it can't be, "I will be real, and I will be me and everything will just happen, Success will find me" We have to understand that there is something bigger than us, something far greater than money or fame. And He wants to do life with us. To me success is doing life with Christ, letting Him guide my steps. That's when we will get our ideas, visions, and purpose. That's when you are successful when you're living on purpose in your purpose.

God knows your desires and every need,
just ask Him to guide your feet. M.M.

As I continue to write this book, God continues to peel off parts of me that no longer serves the woman I am becoming. He is replacing the old me who I once knew to give me a new life that only He knows. When I came to the realization of me being a single mom, I immediately went back to the things I once desired to do but couldn't because of my past relationship. I thought I could get back to me and live how I always wanted to. The funny thing is the vegan food, the responsibility of live plants, yoga, or becoming a Real Estate Agent does not interest me anymore. I always wanted to live a vegan lifestyle because both my parents died from cancer and I thought if I ate well, I would live a long and healthy life, this is true but sometimes it's much deeper than that. The week my ex moved out, I went to the grocery store and spent a great amount of money on vegan food and rid my kitchen of all non-vegan items only to realize the food is not that good to me anymore. In fact, some of it makes me sick to my stomach. I always wanted to do yoga because I was always into doing stretches since taking dance classes in public school. I also have back pains from my first born so I thought yoga would work to tone and heal my muscle pain. I went out and got yoga mats for me and my girls only to realize, once again, that this is totally out of alignment with God and honestly, I'm not that interested in it anymore. I found myself trying to do everything I wanted but still hadn't completed to one thing God had asked me to do since 2019.

Remember in the chapter one, I mentioned God told me to create book and films? Well, allow me to give you the full story. In 2017, I was 25 and was trying to find myself. I was in between the new age phase and serving God. I began to read more, tried yoga here and there, and went vegan for a few months. One of the books I read was Sarah Jakes Roberts – Don't Settle for Safe. One of the main points I received from the book was that God created me with a purpose, He put something in me to serve Him. So, I began to ask God what He created me to do because as far as I am concerned, I am not good at anything, not even yoga. The only problem was, I wasn't ready to leave my relationship or stop drinking. I would literally get intoxicated almost every day, every weekend and get up for church on Sunday like it was nothing, I mean I was taking notes from the pastor and everything. I started this job at a corporate office, and I thought God was answering my prayers. I was so excited, but once I started, I immediately began to understand I was making someone else dream come true, while only making $15 an hour. I begin to understand that I was just an employee working to just pay my bills, drink and take a vacation. Not only that, I also felt completely out of place, there was no one there who looked like me. I remember going to the restroom crying most days because I couldn't afford nice clothes or get my hair done. It became my praying session everyday with God. Then, a thought came to my mind to start an online boutique called Girl with Options, (clears throat) to sell all the things I couldn't afford so I can make money and get the things I wanted. I thought that every woman should have options and look great. We all know now how selfish and narrow minded that was of me. We also know now that that was the birth of something bigger than me. In December of 2018, we moved to NOLA and my plan was to take my income tax check and get all the inventory I needed to open my boutique. I had all of the information I needed and more to start the business. But soon as we moved, my ex and I were out of work for a while and my taxes were used to pay my overdue student loans. I was devastated. I thought I was on my way to generational wealth. I continued to pray, joined a church in early 2019 and started work around July. Even though we were working, and I was a part of a great church, something just was not feeling right within my spirit. One night at bible study, my Pastor did something a little different. He asked everyone to line up and if we had any prayer requests, we could ask, and God would speak. I went up and prayed for my purpose among other things because I understood as long as I have God and I am living in my purpose, everything else would be added unto me. My pastor prayed for me, and my girls and I went home and didn't think anything else about it. Sometime later, I was asleep in my bed and God rose me up and said, "Create books and films based on your experiences." His voice was so calm and pure, but also stern. I knew it was Him, but I just could not understand why He would think I was able to write a book, my handwriting is awful. And what experiences was He talking about exactly? I have terrible handwriting and I would much rather talk about my experiences instead of writing about them. I would much rather be a public speaker or a real estate agent than an author and let's not even talk about films. As time went on, I was more confused than ever. I started to feel like life was passing me by. I started to think how I can live for God, and I am shacking with my kids' father, he doesn't want to go to church or do the things I want to, and I love drinking. Something came over me one day and I explained to him that before we can continue to move forward in our relationship, I need to know if he had been with anyone else besides me. I can't tell you why I asked that, it just hit my spirit. All I know is we had been struggling together for years, trying to make life make sense, and I needed to know this before we continued to do whatever it was that we were doing. Well, his answer was a smirk on his face with a no. You can imagine the argument that turned into. He later explained to me that he was depressed and trying to figure out what he is doing with his life, and he doesn't have time for any other women. I was talking with one of my sisters about how I needed to know if I should stay with him or not. I felt as though something didn't feel right and I needed more in life, what if I am settling? What if there is something greater out there for me? She told me to ask God to reveal His truth and that is exactly what I did. I asked God to fill me with His peace, strength, courage, and endurance. I asked Him to help me to keep going forward to what He has for me, no matter what He may reveal. We'd just moved into our new apartment and things were going well and I honestly forgot about the prayer because things seemed great. I was drinking wine while he and I were laughing and talking about something, and his phone received a notification. It was a woman with a very odd message, which was very interesting because I did not have a phone for a long period of time, and I would constantly use his phone with no problem. I decided to go to the woman's

IG account only to see a picture of a little baby. Something in my spirit led me to ask him if this was his baby. In that moment when he said yes, I could only think, "thank you, God, this is my moment to leave." He continued with the "I don't want her though, I want you" I was extremely calm because now I understand God gave me exactly what I asked for, but I wasn't intentional and allowed myself and the enemy to confuse me. So, you know what I did? I stayed and thought maybe this is my story. Maybe this would be how God would use me and I would be a great stepmom to the baby. He and I would overcome this, and this would be a testimony to share. We started counseling and went to church together twice. I then went back to my girl Sarah Jakes Roberts in December of 2019 and watched her sermon – Girl Get Up. And I knew that message was for me. It reminded me that I have things I needed to do and basically, I am tripping right now. I went home on my lunch break and broke up with him, and you know what he did? He started to name all the things we were doing to become better and how I was leaving too soon. So, yes, I stayed. Looking back, I honestly believe the world had to slow down in 2020 for me to wake the heck up! When we first found out about the shut down due to the pandemic, I was very peaceful and optimistic about the whole thing. I knew God had me and my family and this would be a great time to bond. I began to read again and this time it was a true game changer. His grandfather gifted us with books from our pastor. One is entitled- The Father Daughter Talk and that began to open my eyes to why I was possibly in the relationship to begin with. The other is ~Queenology. Queenology is no joke, I rose up in the middle of reading the book in the same way I did when God spoke to me. By the grace of God, I immediately realized I was wrong, and God answered my prayers and gave me steps, but I was blinded by my own thoughts and desires.

*And we know that all things work
together for good to them that love God,
to them who are the called according
to his purpose. Romans 8:28KJV*

The good news is God is patient and kind and He is standing right where you are with open arms. He will use everything to work out for our good and all who are attached to us. I believe once we give God our yes, and begin to live in our purpose, and turn our back to what we thought we knew, not only are we doing what He is requiring of us, but He will also make room for our desires. And honestly what He has is way better than what we thought we wanted. I believe there is an abundance of possibilities attached to our purpose. I can still invest in property without being a real estate agent. I can still eat and live a healthy lifestyle, I just can't worship vegan food but instead praise God for creating herbs, fruits, and veggies. He is our one and only true provider and healer. God wants to see us happy, healthy, and wealthy; we have an ultimate goal and not just for our selfish wants and needs.

We have to give up all we know in order to follow God and our purpose. This reminds me of the book of Luke when Simon, who was a professional Fisherman, had trouble all night with catching fish. Jesus said to him to let out his net for a catch of fish. Knowing he had been there all night and hadn't caught anything, Simon obeyed and dropped the net only to find that it was more fish than they could bear. He had to call other fishermen to help. He was overwhelmed by what Jesus had done. Jesus told him, "Nothing to fear, from now on you will be a fisherman for women and men." and at that moment Simon dropped everything and followed Him.

When I read this just last week, I was amazed that Simon dropped all he knew to follow Christ. I can only imagine what would have happen if he didn't listen because he was a "professional fisherman"? In the beginning of this chapter, I told you how I wanted to go back to "me" when I became a single mom, but the truth is, that is not who I am or who God has created me to be.

> *Eye hath not seen, nor ear heard, neither have entered into the heart of man, the things which God hath prepared for them that love him. 1 Corinthians 2:9b KJV*

I do not believe He will leave us in a hurtful place. He will fill us and give us way more than what we can ever imagine, we just have to listen. I do believe the saying "when one door closes, another door opens" and I believe that is the door of possibilities, I'm talking about His new opportunities. A lot of times we are selling ourselves short, I'm sure when Simon went out to fish that day, he did not think he would get as many fish as Jesus allowed him to get.

If you are like me, you probably watch Jingle Jangle: A Christmas Journey over and over this past Christmas. I absolutely love the song by Madalen Mills – Square Root of Possible. My daughter and I will sing it to see who can hit the highest note.

We all are Women of Options. We have the options to choose our purpose and destiny, we have the option to choose life and most of all, we have the option to choose Christ. He doesn't force us to do anything, and we do have free will, but once we are ready, He is there. Our purpose is already written, we just have to align ourselves with Him and remember its possible.

I heard another great song today by Bri Babineaux - Love You Forever and it really blessed me. Even on days or weeks when I may mess up, He is still with you and me. He saved me from myself, and I will forever love Him for loving me. He is the father to the fatherless and the mother to the motherless. He is all I need.

Chapter Six

THE OPTION TO CHOOSE LIFE

A dedication to Damian

*How do you help someone who doesn't want to be
helped
How do you save someone who believes they are
trapped*

*Trapped in their mind, believing their existence is a
waste of time
Disgrace, taking up space*

*I wanted to help; I gave you the tools and explained
why Jesus wept
All secrets were kept just needed you to take the first
step
Take Leap of faith, give God a taste
all your sins could have been erased...*

A lot of times we believe it's up to us to save someone but, Jesus is
the one and only true Saviour. All we can do is share our love, light,
and ask God daily to cleanse our hearts. We ask Him to cleanse our
hearts so that we won't become used to living in our selfish ways
and/or ambition. Also, so we won't get trapped in what our culture
labels as normal.

Remember a few chapters back I was expressing how different I am
from my siblings? All my life I used that as my defense magnesium,
an excuse for my selfish ways. A few months ago, I found out my
nephew, who was more like a brother to me, had been struggling for
a long time with depression, anxiety, and dark thoughts. We are a few
years apart and lived together for some time as kids. In that moment

I realized that I was not the only one who felt alone and different. I realized I have been selfish and creating pity parties instead lending a hand to others who may need what I wished I had. I understood my nephew was struggling with his reason for being and his purpose for breathing. That is much deeper than being different from my siblings.

I couldn't see myself giving up on him or treating him any different. I thought maybe he just needed to be reintroduced to God. I explained to him that he was created with a purpose and there is a plan for his life. I expressed to him that he can make it through this with the love and support of our family along with a professional healing treatment. I continued to tell him that his story could be a blessing to someone else and not to give up.

Not long after he expressed his feelings, he started therapy. The entire situation opened my eyes to other things, more than what I was used to before. Six months later, he committed suicide exactly one month before his birthday. He would have been 24 years old. I started to feel as if I had failed him. At the same time, he helped me to understand that I am not the only one who is going through things or the only one who is trying to figure life out. Maybe if I would have caught on to his struggles sooner instead of living in my selfish ways, that option to choose life wouldn't have been so impossible to him. It's not my place to judge, I'm here to simply finish what He had started, to be the bridge for others. I'm here to tell you that no matter what you may be up against, you have options and there is nothing too great or hard for our God. Don't give up and its ok to ask for help and or seek therapy, please don't quit.

With that being said, I dedicate this song to you, Damian and my friend reading this:

I'll Find You by Lecrae ft. Tori Kelly

This book is more than me telling my story, It's a movement. M.M.

The option to choose life is not just about me or you. Choosing life is also about reaching out to that one family member who never says much, they may be struggling more than you think. Choosing life is giving to someone what you feel you are lacking. Lastly, choosing life is forgiving yourself if you didn't understand any of those things until after someone close to you has left. We can't live in pity or regret. We must understand with promotion comes a test and with the testing of our faith, we should ask God to clear whatever is in our hearts that shouldn't be because in the end, our blessings aren't just for us. It reminds me of the saying, "each one, teach one" although this is very true, I would like to say, "each one, reach one". I'm sure if I would have reached for my nephew's hand years ago, this may have ended differently.

I often pray not to become bitter or resentful towards myself because of the decisions I've made. The person who I was is not who I am today or who I'm going to be tomorrow. I also want to take the time to thank God for this moment. I know God makes no mistakes. I would like to think of it as we are in transition; we are in the wilderness and God is bringing us to the promised land. We should remain faithful, intentional, trust in Him, and do the work that He has required of us. Everything is working as it should.

Often times, we think we are in control. Yes, God did give us the freedom of choice and He doesn't force Himself on us, but He is the only one who is really in control. We are taught go to college, pick a career, keep going and never give up. Most of us were never taught to wait on God or how to wait on Him. We are taught to lead by our desires and ambitions and not to seek God for His purpose and/or assignment for our lives. A lot of times we are striving for things in places where God is not present. We must be still and acknowledge God for who He is.

If you don't listen to any of the songs written in this book, please take a moment to listen to Travis Green – Be Still. Because I too, was one who would constantly try different things and would still end up nowhere with nothing to show for it. It wasn't until I decided to be still and listen. That is when I started to hear from God, that's when I became a service to others, and more importantly, that is when I was made new and whole - in silence, in His presence.

We all have options whether they are great or small, good, or bad. We all have the option of doing things our way or seeking Him for the ultimate goal.

"The LORD will fight for you while you [only need to] keep silent and remain calm."

This is one of the reasons I think it was easy for me to finally give up drinking, after being still and listening. Soon after, God revealed to me how empty I was. I needed something to fill me, give me motivation, and make me feel good. I needed something to hide the pain and misery I was living in, the desire of wanting to do more, but not knowing how. Once I was willing to let Him fill me with His Holy Spirit, He took the place of alcohol and filled every void. I don't have the desire to drink because God restored me and revealed to me a new life. I gave up my self-sabotaging ways and replaced drinking, with Him.

I was reading the book of Proverbs where it leads to the Virtuous Woman verse, and I came across this scripture. I would like to share it with you:

"It is not for kings, O Lemuel, it is not for kings to drink wine; nor for princes strong drink: Lest they drink, and forget the law, and pervert the judgment of any of the afflicted. Give strong drink unto him that is ready to perish, and wine unto those that be of heavy hearts. Let him drink, and forget his poverty, and remember his misery no more." Proverbs 31:4-7 KJV

I was astounded when I read this passage. I never paid it any attention before. It made so much sense to me in that very moment. I was using other things to stimulate me instead of reaching for the one and only true God to heal me. It's funny because I was the reason I was in that place, because I thought I was in control instead of laying all my burdens at His feet.

Sometimes we are looking for the exact answer or the step-by-step experiences of others but sometimes we have to just go for it. When all else fails, we must lay all we know aside and go to Him. Your story is not like anyone else's, and God may not get your attention the way He did others. When you look at your options and decide to choose God, remember it's not going to be perfect. It's not always a day of roses, but even if it was, each rose has its own prickles and prickles serve to keep away predators. Sometimes we are our own predators and there will be moments when you hurt, nevertheless God is with you. You can get through it. Remember, when you get to those moments, it is okay to take a day off to spend time alone with you and God.

Above I mentioned how God restored me and took the place of alcohol. If you were like me a few months ago, you may be asking what is restoration and how do you obtain it?

Restoration - is to receive back more than has been lost to the point where the final state is greater than the original condition. The main point is that someone or something is improved beyond measure. - Google

In my experience, in order to be restored, the first step is we must want to be in God's presence. (That's were those options comes in.) Again, He will never force Himself on us. He should be something we want and someone whom we want to be in relationship with. I know that there are some people who say, "it wasn't their choice" or they did not have "this" in mind or "God chose them." This is true and honest. I believe He chose all of us for something. But I believe the ones who were "unexpectedly chosen" still had to be open to God at some point in their lives. They had to answer the call and be sensitive towards Him. That's where the restoration begins, by choosing to be open, just a little, be submissive and when He knocks, we are sensitive to the call. It is in our "yes" when He will literally give us the game plan, we just have to open our hearts.

Second, make time for Him. The best thing we can do during the time of restoration is sit in silence. He will then open your eyes to things you've ignored in the past. Use that time to ask for forgiveness, thank Him for being God, and thank Him for the good, bad and the ugly. Things are not going to be easier because God restored you, however you will have a new level of strength and courage about you.

Third, make time for reading the Bible. Ask the Holy spirit to read with you. This changed everything for me because honestly the bible is not the easiest book to read. It's amazes me each time I am worried about something, I find my answer in my daily word. I recommend a study bible because it breaks down each scripture and gives you a better insight of each verse.

And lastly, my favorite, be intentional. You will begin to see how things in the past came together for this very moment in time. Going forward we must be mindful of the things we are doing and our why.

Once God restored me, He restored my faith and trust in Him as well. This reminds me of times before I would be in church and feel embarrassed when I didn't have tithe money. It was always a desire of mine to be a blessing, contributor, and sow seeds. I knew there was more in return for my ten percent, and I always wanted to pay tithes but never knew where to start. Think about it, you get paid on Friday, you spent all your money on Saturday, church is on Sunday, and the pastor says, "give the Lord ten percent." I would be thinking, "I spent that on my daiquiris and crawfish." – trying to hold on to my last $100 because I didn't trust God enough. But it was in those moments, when I was in the presence of God during the pandemic, I said I have tried everything else, let me try it God's way. I have been faithfully paying tithes ever since.

> There comes a time in our lives when
> we have to just go for it. M.M.

Woman of Options means, we are entitled to more than what we have been taught or conditioned to believe. We have the option to serve a great God. We have the option to wait, seek, and listen to Him, after all He will restore all that was lost. We have the option of doing more than working a 9-5, living paycheck to paycheck, and retire. We have the option of doing great things in this world, but it's not about feeding our ambition, pleasing our desires or selfish needs. We have the option to be all we were created to be and bless others along the way. But first, we must choose to seek our creator.

Don't be afraid of the unknown or the change that comes with seeking God and living in your purpose. I promise you, there is greater on the other side of fear and worry. Remember who you are: A child of God and we are not slaves to fear. This brings me to Tasha Cobbs Leonard – No Longer Slaves, listen to it when you get the chance.

Chapter Seven

WE KNOW WHO WE ARE

When I meet the world, I am not asking who I am; I am introducing myself because I know who I am from my soul – RC Blakes, Jr

I know I've stated in the last chapter we should not be driven by our own desires and ambitions. But now that we understand our blessings are not only for us and we understand the importance of having a clean heart, let's go back to our desires, passions, and purpose. Revisit your dreams, thoughts, or notes. Revisit your vision board if you must so you can get back to your purpose. Our desires, passion, and purpose are not our own, meaning it did not come from us. God gave it to us. So, it is OK to embrace it with a clean heart and understand that the blessings attached to it are not only for us but for the glory of God. As I stated in previous chapters, I always wanted to be a Real Estate agent. I also had a desire of being a successful businesswoman. When God called me to write this book, I understood that my gifts would make room for me. I understood that God makes no mistakes, so I can obey Him and know He will make a way for me to do all the things I want to do. Lastly, I understood His purpose and plan for my life is far greater than anything I could ever imagine. I believe He will take what we want and make it grand so it would be a blessing for me, you, and others all while giving Him all the glory, honor, and praise. I do tend to get off track sometimes and try to do things my way. I may try to rush the process or take a detour. Times like those have proven to me that if I continue down His right path, I will be able to do the things I desire, and it will be more impactful in the end. The season we are in now is preparing us for our debut to the world.

*A man's gift [given in love or courtesy]
makes room for him And brings him
before great men Proverbs 18:16 AMP*

I've always had an idea of being on stage whether I was speaking, acting, or something of that nature. I even had a small idea of writing a book a few years ago (before God confirmed it) but I was never motivated or believed I had anything worth saying. And honestly, I was driven by money during that time. Now I understand those thoughts were not mine alone. After God started doing the work in me (He still doing the work in me as I speak) I realized that it's OK to have the desire to want to be successful, speak on stage, or to be well known. After all, if we thought of it then God called us to do it in some shape or form which means we need to execute at some point. Every thought and or idea came from Him. I believe that is why sometimes we may go through different challenges, trials, and tribulation – to qualify us and our faith. I realized now writing was not my own thought. He has a bigger plan for you and me. So, let's begin to live in what we were called to do. We are now breaking up with our past and completing this chapter with Grace. We are moving forward with the knowledge and understanding of our future. We're letting go of fear and we're going to move in faith and favor. We know who we are, and the time is now to start owning it. We have spent enough time on things that were keeping us stagnant. God did not create us to be stuck. We can't continue to focus on anything or anyone that is not related to our purpose. We know who we are, so let's get to work. There were moments in my life I would have labeled myself as the Queen of procrastination. I would wait until the very last minute and then do the bare minimum. Behavior like that has not done anything progressive in my life but made me a progressive procrastinator. Today, I understand the actions I take now will determine how my children and grandchildren will live and behave later.

The world needs what you have to offer. M.M.

> *Do you understand how beautiful you are?*
> *How great you are?*
> *No one could be you even if they tried.*
> *God did this on purpose, He knew what He was doing*
> *when He created you...*

Understand, God knows the desires of your heart and He knows our needs. I believe you will get all your heart's desire, you are successful, and you are no longer afraid, I speak this over you. We are no longer living in fear, shame, or doubt. In fact, it is time to close the chapter of shame. Ashamed to stand tall in your purpose, ashamed of being an independent woman because you don't want to offend anyone and ashamed of saying what you mean and meaning what you say. Jonathan McReynolds said it best, I'm moving on.

> *I'm closing chapters*
> *I'm turning pages*
> *Glory to glory*
> *And from faith to favor*
>
> *I'm moving on*

When God delivers us, He doesn't do it for us to stay in the same position where He found us. M.M

Moving on is not always the easiest thing to do because at times we tend to get comfortable. We are survivors at heart, and we adapt quickly. We adapt to the conditions which we are in. We forget that there is a higher calling for our lives. We forget how God has brought us through and now we must continue to move and grow closer to Him. Although we are survivors it can be beauty and a curse. It's beauty because by the Grace of God, we are survivors. We can make it through anything, we can handle all things through Christ. We learn to make the best of our situation. It can become a curse when we master being in awkward positions. We master being at the bottom of the pit when we should continue to fight and keep moving from glory to glory. If I'm honest, I'll have to admit to feeling stuck ever since I have decided to write this book. Somewhere along the way I became used to my circumstances instead of being in a constant need for Him. I took pride in God delivering me from sex and alcohol as if that was the end all be all. I stayed there until I eventually I became distinct. Once I realized I was out of synch, I wanted to go back to the very moment and feeling in which, He first saved me. After watching my girl, Sarah, I began to understand more that I couldn't go back to that moment because he already delivered me from it. Now, I must go to the next level in God. As Sarah stated, we need "a new tone", I need a new word from Him, I need Him to deliver or heal me from the "next". I love how God will take our mistakes and make it a blessing. Although I dislike the feeling of being distant from Him, I am grateful to be able to share all of my experiences with you. I am sharing this not to discourage you, but to inform you that all of this is normal for all to need a revival at some point. As I was sitting with this, I decided to google the word revival and noticed that was exactly what I needed.

The word "revival" is from the Hebrew word chayah and means "to bring back to life". As stated in the Bible, it means rejuvenation or renewal of interest after spiritual neglect. -Google

---

We will never come to a place of arrival and no longer need Him. M.M.

God convicted me on this a few weeks ago. I found myself getting too comfortable with what He has called me to do that I'd begin to not rely solely on Him. Even though we may be doing what God has called us to do and we are still healing from our past, we can't forget this one thing: We still need Him in order to do what He has called us to do. There will never come a time when we don't need Him. God revealed to me that there will never come a time when I am so holy or delivered that I won't need Him anymore to guide me. So just because He told me to write books, doesn't mean I can take Him for granted and not completely depend on him.

2 years ago, I left my life as I knew it in Chicago and moved to NOLA. I began to let go of everything that was keeping me from depending on God. Once I did this, my breakthrough came. M.M.

I was sitting in Walmart parking lot one day listening to Tasha Cobbs Leonard's, Sense It and I thought about my relationship with God and how it had changed over the years. One thing that I love about Him is that I can be myself completely and He will still hear me and give me direction. For this, I love my relationship with Him. The fact that I cannot dance nor sing, I still enjoy worshipping God, and He hears and enjoy me as well. I mean, don't you love how you can be yourself; you can sing to God, you can rap to God, and you can talk to Him the same way you would talk to your friends, and He still hears you and loves you. Even if you may not be intentional (yet) with your prayers, your relationship with Him, or you don't fully know what you are called to do, you can still have this great relationship with Him. You may not know the full meaning of submitting and letting God lead and guide you to your divine purpose (YET), but He always has a way of reaching His people. I know because all of this was me. So, if you are unsure, just keep praising and worshipping because He is about to answer you. I don't know about you, but I can sense something great is about to happen. I can sense something new is in the atmosphere. I believe we are about to receive all that has been promised to us. I can sense it, you are changing and becoming more every day.

We've got history. M.M.

The first time I ever heard this song, I was working for a company that I didn't like too much. I began to repeat Tasha stating, "make me a miracle, I'll be the miracle". not fully understanding what that meant exactly, but I knew I was to the point where I wanted whatever God had for me and I was willing to endure it all for it. Little did I know, a year later I would become pregnant, have the idea of Woman of Options, move away from my family, end a 11-year relationship, and lose my nephew all to the miracle of God. All of this and more has been very challenging but I constantly ask myself, "if He was keeping me when I was wrong, why wouldn't He keep me while I'm serving Him intentionally?" This is something we all should think about. We must get to the place where we say, "Father, I trust you and I will surrender to your will. Its time I put all my trust in you because you are my provider and perfect help. I must believe you have something greater for me. And I also believe you won't let me fall nor fail. Please forgive me for thinking anything other than that." Yes, sometimes things do happen that are unexpected, but we can expect God to use it for our good and show up just like He always has. We can expect that in the end, we will be better and stronger than before. So, lets end this chapter with a declaration that something good is coming to us. Let's also remember to be in a constant need of Him, wait on Him, and not be moved by our emotions or the state of the world.

> But they that wait upon the Lord shall renew their strength; they shall mount up with wings as eagles; they shall run, and not be weary; and they shall walk, and not faint. Isaiah 40:31KJV

Say this with me:

- *I'm a queen*
- *I'm am fearfully and wonderfully made, marvelous Are thy works*
- *I'm the head and not the tail.*
- *I'm above and not beneath -I'm a lender and not a borrower*
- *God made me on purpose with a purpose in my mind.*

Remember, God intentionally made you, so go be intentional with your purpose. Now go pick up your crown.

Listen to the song whenever you need a little reminder that you and Him have history, meaning He will not leave you nor forsake you, just hold tight.

Epilogue

FROM NEW AGE TO NEW BEGINNINGS

As we end, let's have a moment of transparency. Woman of Options is a movement of God. This is a safe place. We cannot be healed, changed, or prosper if we are not open and honest. Here is a scripture from Proverbs 28:13:

> He that covereth his sins shall not prosper:
> but whoso confesseth and forsaketh them
> shall have mercy. Proverbs 28:13KJV

See, your girl was almost in the "New Age" community, ok! I want to share this with you because I honestly thought it was normal and I know there are others who may think it is normal too. I always believed in God and had a prayer life. But somewhere along the way, I became distant from the holy spirit, somewhere between facing my wounds and burying them. See, we cannot bury our wounds and forget about them. We must face them with God on our side, heal from them and let the wounds serve us. Your wounds are what make you relatable, knowledgeable, and wise. I thought I was in control of my life and all pertaining to it. I believed if I had good intentions, God would bless whatever I prayed for. I tried my best to put God in things I knew deep down was not of Him. I believed if I put out "good energy/vibes" I would receive "good energy/vibes" and I would be in control of my day. We all know this is not true. There are days we wake up with good intentions and will still receive a negative response or "vibe" from someone who may not be at peace with themselves. We cannot control that. Therefore, it is important to seek and acknowledge the Holy Spirit and ask for peace that surpass all understanding. I believed I was "spiritual" and was free to decide what to believe and how to use it accordingly in my life. I attempted (and failed) a vegan lifestyle to live longer and healthier. If my kids or I would become sick I could "heal" us with God's herbs, fruits, and vegetables. I begin to study essential oils and its properties for healing as well. I also started wearing waist beads which is said to have healing, spiritual and fertility qualities. As I may have mentioned in recent chapters, there is nothing wrong with being vegan, vegetarian, keto or whatever you may choose. In fact, I love and still use essential oils to this day, the issue is when we think we are in control of our bodies to the point we unconsciously think we are healers instead of relying on God. Yes, we all should eat right and be little healthier but there is only one true Healer, and He fills us with discernment and wisdom to make better choices through Him.

We can't do anything without the Holy Spirit. M.M.

I attempted to try yoga for a more holistic lifestyle to go along with eating right, transformation and healing. I believed I could heal my aches and pains from my pregnancies while also clearing my thoughts so I could figure out my purpose, which led me to becoming interested in un-biblical meditation. Although I was afraid to try it, it was something I liked about "self-manifestation, selfcare and focusing on the future you", which now, I know are all lies. All those things I named was about Y.O.U. Which means I was making myself the center of everything like I had all power in my hands. With every blessing, test, trial, and tribulation we face, it is not just about us or for us. This life is not our own and we have to know the true word of God, so we won't be deceived. As far as self-care, I don't see anything wrong with it, but I believe we should be more in tuned with our "soul-care". I think now is the time to become more sanctified which means set apart for God. We must be careful of what the world labels as selfcare and not be conformed to it. I do believe in taking time to do things you like or things that make you feel more like a woman like getting a massage or getting your nails done, but let's not forget about our soul work with the Lord. I don't know about you, but when I finish my worship songs, praying and crying with God, I feel refreshed, new, and clean. I feel like I can conquer the world. To me, that's true "self-care".

Jesus is Self-care. M.M.

I thank God, He did not let me go or take his hand off me. There were some things I knew I just could not do, like sage and un-godly meditations to name a few. I do believe that most of my mistakes were because of my rebellious ways but I also believe it is a testimony to help other girls and women like me. The enemy is working hard to confuse us. New age for some seems innocent because you may have good vibes, mindful eating habits and mediate. But the word says to mediate on the word of God and to keep our minds stayed on thee. Worldly meditations ask you to clear your mind completely and "center your thoughts". That's some scary stuff, how can I center my thoughts on my future when I am not my own, I am not my creator? Remember, an idle mind is the devil workshop. When our minds are blank, that is an easy access for all things other than God. The enemy can sneak in and confuse us real quick. But when we keep our focus on the word of the Lord, we will begin to believe His word is true and that's the real manifestation. God wants to see us all win. He created us to win but He also wants to do life with us. We should never forget who He is and try to do things our way, it will only lead to destruction. Listen, I know it may be difficult for someone who is not used to reading the bible or praying to keep their mind on the word of God, but if you could at lease start off with one small scripture to repeat and memorize it, that's enough, God will handle the rest.

We must focus on the word of the Lord and seek Him for guidance. M.M.

All of this was a part of His plan, and all the glory is His. What you are going through is not in vain. It is to strengthen, teach and prepare you for the next. We should never be ashamed of the choices we have made in the past or challenges we have faced. We must constantly be in the state of learning and growing through Christ. In my personal experiences, I wasn't taught certain things, so I grew to have the "I know it all mentality" which eventually caused me to become humble after I realized I had things completely wrong. It also cost me some valuable time, but I believe God will restore all of the time lost. It also caused me to want to reach out to a community of women who are like me so we can teach, lead, and push each other to purpose with grace, wisdom, love, and prayer.

This is only the beginning. M.M.

I pray this book blesses you as much as it has blessed me to write it. I would like to thank you for taking the time to read and making it to the end of the book. I want you to know that this is only the beginning for you. I may not know you personally, but I still believe great things are in store for you and you will make it through. Remember, it will not be easy just because you gave God your yes, in fact I cried while writing majority of this book, but it is well worth it. God is waiting for you to step into your greatness. Get up, girl because you have OPTIONS!

*With God and your faith, all
things are possible! M.M.*

I would like to leave with you some scriptures to help you through your journey. Once I gave God my yes, the attack from the enemy came like never before. The good news is that means your blessing is on the way. So, whenever you are feeling defeated, anxious, or feeling nothing at all, please refer to the following verses and meditate on them. They have helped me make it through some tuff times and I believe it will bless you too.

If you have trouble understanding scriptures like I once did, here are some tips I have tried myself: Number 1, Pray and invite the holy spirit to read with you. Number 2, get a study bible. Number 3, get the bible app and try reading in the King James Version (all listed below) and then read in The Message version (or any other you may choose). This way you can compare the different language for a better understating. Number 4, Google the scripture you are having trouble with. There are a lot of Christian blogs that explain the scripture and goes into more of the details. You can try all four tips in order as they are listed, I still do them to this very day.

Healing:

James 5:15

"and the prayer of faith shall save the sick, and the Lord shall raise him up; and if he have committed sins, they shall be forgiven him."

Psalm 107:20

"Surely he hath borne our griefs, and carried our sorrows: yet we did esteem him stricken, smitten of God, and afflicted. But he was wounded for our transgressions, he was bruised for our iniquities: the chastisement of our peace was upon him; and with his stripes we are healed."

Proverbs 4:20-22

"My son, attend to my words; Incline thine ear unto my sayings. Let them not depart from thine eyes; Keep them in the midst of thine heart. For they are life unto those that find them, And health to all their flesh."

Psalm 103:3-5

"Who forgiveth all thine iniquities; Who healeth all thy diseases; Who redeemeth thy life from destruction; Who crowneth thee with lovingkindness and tender mercies; Who satisfieth thy mouth with good things; So that thy youth is renewed like the eagle's."

Trusting God and His timing:

Proverbs 3:5-6

"Trust in the LORD with all thine heart; and lean not unto thine own understanding. [6] In all thy ways acknowledge him, and he shall direct thy paths.

Romans 8:28

And we know that all things work together for good to them that love God, to them who are the called according to his purpose.

Psalms 118:24

This is the day which the Lord hath made; we will rejoice and be glad in it.

Isaiah 40:31

But they that wait upon the LORD shall renew their strength; they shall mount up with wings as eagles; they shall run, and not be weary; and they shall walk, and not faint.

Isaiah 55:11

So shall my word be that goeth forth out of my mouth: it shall not return unto me void, but it shall accomplish that which I please, and it shall prosper in the thing whereto I sent it.

Restoration:

Psalms 51:10

Create in me a clean heart, O God; and renew a right spirit within me.

Jeremiah 30:17

For I will restore health unto thee, and I will heal thee of thy wounds, saith the LORD; because they called thee an Outcast, saying, This is Zion, whom no man seeketh after.

Psalm 51:12

Restore unto me the joy of thy salvation; and uphold me with thy free spirit.

Psalm 139:23-24

Search me, O God, and know my heart: try me, and know my thoughts: And see if there be any wicked way in me, and lead me in the way everlasting.

1 Peter 5:10

But the God of all grace, who hath called us unto his eternal glory by Christ Jesus, after that ye have suffered a while, make you perfect, stablish, strengthen, settle you."

Purpose (the option to choose life):

Deuteronomy 30:19

I call heaven and earth to record this day against you, that I have set before you life and death, blessing and cursing: therefore choose life, that both thou and thy seed may live:

Matthew 6:33

But seek ye first the kingdom of God, and his righteousness; and all these things shall be added unto you.

Joshua 1:8

This book of the law shall not depart out of thy mouth; but thou shalt meditate therein day and night, that thou mayest observe to do according to all that is written therein: for then thou shalt make thy way prosperous, and then thou shalt have good success.

Hebrews 10:23

Let us hold fast the profession of our faith without wavering; (for he is faithful that promised;)

Jeremiah 1:5

Before I formed thee in the belly I knew thee; and before thou camest forth out of the womb I sanctified thee, and I ordained thee a prophet unto the nations.

Anxiety, Fear, Worry:

Philippians 4:6-7 NKJV

Be anxious for nothing, but in everything by prayer and supplication, with thanksgiving, let your requests be made known to God; [7] and the peace of God, which surpasses all understanding, will guard your hearts and minds through Christ Jesus.

II Timothy 1:7

For God hath not given us the spirit of fear; but of power, and of love, and of a sound mind.

Matthew 11:28-30

Come unto me, all ye that labour and are heavy laden, and I will give you rest. Take my yoke upon you, and learn of me; for I am meek and lowly in heart: and ye shall find rest unto your souls. For my yoke is easy, and my burden is light.

Acts 16:31

And they said, Believe on the Lord Jesus Christ, and thou shalt be saved, and thy house.

James 1:2-4

My brethren, count it all joy when ye fall into divers temptations; Knowing this, that the trying of your faith worketh patience. But let patience have her perfect work, that ye may be perfect and entire, wanting nothing.

Strength and Courage:

Joshua 1:9

Have not I commanded thee? Be strong and of a good courage; be not afraid, neither be thou dismayed: for the LORD thy God is with thee whithersoever thou goest.

Philippians 4:13

I can do all things through Christ which strengtheneth me.

Proverbs 18:10

The name of the LORD is a strong tower: the righteous runneth into it, and is safe.

Romans 5:3

And not only so, but we glory in tribulations also: knowing that tribulation worketh patience;

Tithing, Sowing, Finances:

Malachi 3:10

Bring ye all the tithes into the storehouse, that there may be meat in mine house, and prove me now herewith, saith the LORD of hosts, if I will not open you the windows of heaven, and pour you out a blessing, that there shall not be room enough to receive it.

Luke 6:38

> Give, and it shall be given unto you; good measure, pressed down, and shaken together, and running over, shall men give into your bosom. For with the same measure that ye mete withal it shall be measured to you again.

II Corinthians 9:7

> Every man according as he purposeth in his heart, so let him give; not grudgingly, or of necessity: for God loveth a cheerful giver.

Galatians 6:7

> Be not deceived; God is not mocked: for whatsoever a man soweth, that shall he also reap.

Mark 4:26-27

> And he said, So is the kingdom of God, as if a man should cast seed into the ground; And should sleep, and rise night and day, and the seed should spring and grow up, he knoweth not how.

II Corinthians 9:10

> Now he that ministereth seed to the sower both minister bread for your food, and multiply your seed sown, and increase the fruits of your righteousness;)

II Corinthians 9:8

> And God is able to make all grace abound toward you; that ye, always having all sufficiency in all things, may abound to every good work:

Proverbs 22:7

> The rich ruleth over the poor, and the borrower is servant to the lender.

Luke 14:28-30

For which of you, intending to build a tower, sitteth not down first, and counteth the cost, whether he have sufficient to finish it? Lest haply, after he hath laid the foundation, and is not able to finish it, all that behold it begin to mock him, Saying, This man began to build, and was not able to finish.

About the Author

Moniquea Matthews, who is affectionally known as "Monique" is a native of McComb, Mississippi. She is the "baby" of eight.

Growing up, Moniquea considered herself to honest, talkative, kind and all about change. She was the only one who was not afraid to ask her dad anything while everyone else stayed out of his way. This is what made her knowledgeable and aware of her family gifts and curses. Most of her family is the "don't ask, don't tell" type, but she believes, that kind of mentality is what causes us to keep cycles going instead of healing from them. She credits her dad for her considering herself a boss and her desire to open several businesses. He is also part of the reason why it has taken a while for her to begin to share her story.

Her mom was her best friend. She was so peaceful, kind and what she believes to be her personal angel.

After her mother passed away, she felt like a piece of her left as well. She could not find anything that made her feel motivated. She failed to understand that she needed to heal and seek God more.

Moniquea decided to become a mother. She wanted to give love to someone the same way her mother loved her. Her beautiful daughter, Nevaeh Angel Robinson was born two years and two months after her mother passed. She was trying to fill a void instead of asking God to fill her.

A short time after her daughter was born, her father passed away. She was a single mom trying to find her way.

After spending some time in Chicago with her oldest sister, she moved to New Orleans and added a beautiful baby girl named Marley Leilani Love Robinson to her family.

She is now living every day, intentionally seeking God and focused on healing and submitting to God. She feels at peace because this is the first time in her life, she is alone, with God and her girls and she is enjoying it.

Moniquea is the Founder/CEO of Woman of Options. She frequently uses Instagram and YouTube as her personal blog to reach women who are just like her.

God told her a year ago to create books and films to share her experiences. There is more to Moniquea, this is only the beginning, and she is ready for the ride.

Connect with Moniquea Matthews and Woman of Options:

Website: www.moniqueamatthews.com
Email: info@moniqueamatthews.com

Instagram-Moniquea Matthews
Facebook-Moniquea Matthews
YouTube-Moniquea Matthews
Twitter-Moniquea Matthews

Made in the USA
Coppell, TX
03 December 2021